# Ecommerce Website With WooCommerce -Build an ecommerce Store

# Section 1: Introduction

# Introduction

Hello and welcome. what I want to do right now is to give you a quick overview of what's inside this book of course. That way you're gonna get a bird's eye view of the whole book as a whole. we'll talk about themes because the design and the look is really important especially to the customer especially how you lay things out and all that. So we're gonna show you where to go to get access to woo commerce themes that are already premade for you. That way you don't have to create it from scratch or hire anyone to create it from scratch and you can simply purchase it download it upload it and you're good to go. And we'll talk about the general settings within Wu commerce and then exactly how to tweak them how to customize them. Also we'll talk about the product settings overview which are the products how to create a product how to edit a product how to customize a product. Once you've created your products you want to make sure that you organize them because you never know if you will add more in the future and especially if you start creating 10 20 30 or more. It can be come very disorganized. So you want to make sure that you create a an organized system. So we'll teach you how to organize things and how to utilize the options with built in Wu commerce to organize your products so that it makes it easier not only for you to find for also your customer to find as well. we'll talk about the product attributes product attributes are basically like if you were to buy a skateboard and you want it in green blue purple different colors maybe different shapes different wheels. That is what we call product attributes. And of course we'll talk about expansion what we mean by that is how do you go beyond the core foundation. Let's say for example that you want to run subscriptions or you want to expand on that. You want to do marketing you want install a different aspects beyond just the basics. So how do you go about doing that . We'll talk about how to automate tedious Woo commerce tasks. Let's say for example that after somebody purchases an item you want to add them to a Google spreadsheet or add them to your list or you want to do something very specific that takes a lot of time. Something that you can't really be there 24/7 to actually do. So in other words once you have set up these automation is then it's going to make your life a lot easier. The more you automate the more you can actually focus on marketing your store getting people to your store and to focus on other things. OK. So what I want to talk about right now is what you need before you can get started. So before we even dive into the book you are going to need these things. So obviously you're going to need a Web site with Wordpress already installed now in terms of where you need to figure out if you want your store located on a subdomain such as store dot your domain dot com. Or maybe you want it to be located within a sub folder such as your domain dot com slash store or within the main site. So those are things that you need to figure out before you read this book of course. Now obviously you can read the book of course and then go back and implement that as well. But the main thought process is where do you want to install. So most people just install Woo commerce wherever their WordPress site is located . So if that's the case you don't really need to worry about that. I just wanted to mention that as an option because that way you can segment your main site and your store if you choose to do so. But otherwise if you don't really care you can install it wherever your WordPress is installed. Now there's a lot of courses a lot of videos out there on the basics of WordPress. You can find a lot on YouTube or other platforms as well. And sometimes you can find them for free on the basics of installing Wordpress and sometimes you can get your web hosting company to do that for you as well. Once you have figured that out the next step is why. So why are you creating your store. You need to understand the purpose and the goal behind your site is it to make a certain amount of money. Is it to obviously everyone wants to make money but is it to impact a certain amount of people or is it to sell. Let's say you have a warehouse and you have 100 skateboards or hundred of something and you want to get rid of that. So what is the purpose you want to write that down. Because you want to figure out in months time after you set up your woo commerce site. If you've actually reach those goals. So this is kind of a little bit of goal setting but you really need to figure that out before you actually start yours site because as you start your store you can begin to implement things that will actually help build upon that and help you reach that goal. If that makes sense and of course the what. What covers an idea or my map of how you want your site to look like. And of course to work together. So basically you want to connect the dots. Figure out what your site needs to do. There are many different mind map soft wares out there you go to Google type in a free mind map software or my map software or flowchart software whatever you want to do. We like lucid chart dot com. That's another good option. It does cost a little bit of money but it's a really good tool to organize your thoughts. So what I'm getting at here is there's a lot of thoughts in your head that you just need to get down on paper. All right. So last but not least the how is this book. So now that you have a good idea of what you need before you can actually implement Woo commerce. Let's jump in and talk about commerce themes.

# Section 2: Lets build your store

# Learn about themes and where

we're going to talk about where you can go to get Woo commerce themes. So a lot of you might be thinking OK where do I get a theme that looks like maybe something of my industry or my target market so that I don't have to design it from scratch. See back in the day you would have to design it from scratch. But nowadays there are hundreds if not thousands of woo commerce themes that you can pick and choose from. So going back to why you want to create your store and what niche you want to create your store for those are crucial things to have in mind as you begin to look for Woo commerce themes. So what I'm going to do now is just show you different sites that you can go to get where commerce themes. The first one is called template monster dot com. That's template monster dot com template monster has been around since themes were even created when themes were beginning to be created. Initially many decades ago. So they have tons and tons of different themes that you can pick and choose from. Now there are tons of themes and bear in mind that there are many themes that are not compatible to WordPress. So you need to look for a woo commerce theme or make sure that the theme is compatible to that platform because there are many themes that are compatible to a variety of different platforms. So you need to keep that in mind as you look at different themes. So if you go to the site and up at the top you click on icon you'll see under Web site templates wordpress themes with commerce themes and elements for Marketplace. So the difference between wordpress themes and with commerce themes is WordPress simply encompasses everything WordPress Woo commerce on the other hand will look like an actual store. That's why you need to figure out do you want it on a subdomain or do you want it on a small folder. Some people will realize this when they begin to install the theme that OK you have a blog. You have different content on the main site whereas the store is totally different. So when you go to woo commerce themes they're obviously going to look like an e-commerce store. template monster has 791 new commerce themes. As of now of course that number will grow beyond later down the road. is a list of the Web commerce themes. You can see the different designs and all that. Now I want to say if you want to focus on a target market and you want that theme to be designed around that target market you can search for that target market. So let's say for example books so we don't know necessarily if there's a theme for books but let's just do a search so we look at this and we think OK we have a e-commerce store that is focused on books. Now this is great because it gives you an idea of what is possible. And if you just want to start out of the gate and you don't really want to think Can you just want to start uploading your products and that's it.

This is the best technique to apply. All right. So books different categories different niches just type that in and do a search and find the theme that you like and go for it. Now I want to say you may find free will commerce themes out there but I want to caution you because a lot of those themes and I won't say all of those things but some of themes have viruses or they're merely released for free so that they can link back to the creator site and there's nothing wrong with that in terms of back links. But as a business owner if you're trying to run a business you want to run a good business. You want to make sure that the Web commerce theme is updated constantly. So at the end of the day you want to make sure that you choose a theme that cost a little bit of money. The reason why we caution you against free themes not necessarily all the time viruses but even if they are clean because they are free long term wise and long term view they may shut down. All right. So another thing you want to think about when you find a theme is the theme developed by a reputable vendor. Now you won't really know that unless you do a little bit of research. So if you go for example and let's say we want to choose maybe the one up so we click details and template monster what they'll do is as you scroll down it says it's 94 bucks and you can get it a lot cheaper at different sites . But if you scroll down this is what it looks like we can see intro benefits reviews a lot of times I like to go to reviews to see if other people have purchased it because just because the theme looks nice doesn't always mean that it's going to work properly. The reviews and the comments are great because it'll tell you if there are problems with theme. So we notice that there are no reviews and no comments for theme. If we do a search on a different theme and we see a lot of reviews we still see a lot of comments that say something like Oh this is a really good easy install. That is something that you might want to go forward with. But if you look at the reviews and comments and they say this theme I installed it I had a lot of problems I spent hours I couldn't figure out and you don't see support actually responding then that's sure fire. No reason just stay away from particular theme. So you really need to do your diligence beyond just picking and choosing a theme. Now one site in several sites that you can choose first of all is commerce. So woo commerce dot com that's the main site which is by WordPress. If you go to the theme store and all themes most of the time and pretty much the majority ninety nine point nine percent or even 100 percent. themes are guaranteed to work because it's developed by a reputable company. It's developed by Woo commerce themselves. So you simply select theme store you can see there's different industries so you can pick and choose the industry that matches you. And that's what I recommend that you do. So if you scroll down and let's say for example that we do something like software so we scroll down further and take a look at what they have. Take a look at the demo so you can get an idea of what is possible. Now I want to say even though the theme might be for a specific niche it doesn't necessarily mean that it's going to be targeted just for that need. You can take something that's dealing with arts and crafts and of course change it to something like electronics or books and so forth. You don't have to be tied to that but I'm just showing you this method just because it's easier. Now another site that you can go to is called theme forest dot net. That's been forest dot net and theme forest on net is owned by a company called in vato and in Votto has been around for a long time. The point that you can literally find hundreds and hundreds of themes in a lot of these actually have comments and actually have reviews . The reason why I want to show you the template monster was simply because I wanted to show you the different avenues and the different options that you have. So if you scroll down we can see different themes that are compatible with commerce. You can see that there's a lot of themes here that look really nice. Now one method that I like to take is after I do a search on say e-commerce themes or woo commerce themes so you can go to WordPress and go to e-commerce and most likely these fit with commerce but you got to double check as well because there's a thousand three hundred twenty two were press Woo commerce themes but there's also themes that are compatible to cart 66 or jigger shop. So these may not necessarily be compatible to woo commerce. They always rank it by sales so you can see this theme has been sold 100000 thousand times or 36000 times or 12000 times. This gives us a good reason that OK if people are buying many people bought it then the theme has less problems than the theme is being updated. So let's say that we want to choose this one . So comparatively to template monster as you can see 100 bucks versus you know 30 to 50 dollars theme forest is definitely cheaper. So if you scroll down you can see that one theme can actually fit many different niches. It doesn't have to be necessarily one niche but sometimes if you find a theme that focuses on one niche it will actually create solutions that will fit that one niche. All right. So that's the advantage of finding a theme that fits one niche. Now this is sort of like a one size fits all. All right. So we got 4.0 would mark this one. A lot of physical products but I see if it's many niches now the one thing that you want to make sure of when you look for a will commerce theme is it easy to set up. So this one they market a visual drag and drop header layout builder. So that's a good sign. If you want to just simply drag and drop things and set things up really easily and quickly so as we scroll down we're seeing a lot of different features a lot of different benefits and different features different plug ins that are included so I want to say when you find a theme that you really like and you want to do some due diligence what you want to do is you want to go all the way down to the bottom and it will show you what we call a change log the change log basically tells you how many times or how much the theme has been updated. Actually a few weeks ago. But we can see that every update has a ton of different features so that's a good sign. So if we scroll back to the top we can see what it is compatible with. So it's compatible with commerce three point eight three point seven three point six. And it's also compatible with Wordpress five point three. Five point two five went and 5.0. So what that tells us is this is updated frequently and that's a good sign. So beyond the sales if we take a look at the comments what we're looking is are the comments in are the questions being resolved and responded to. Is there a way to rearrange the order of the product attributes and the author has responded during the same day. Sometimes you might find a theme that is being sold but the author is not responding. So that's a problem because if you run into a problem into the authors not communicating with you then you're going to run into that roadblock and you'll have lose some money. So that's why I say find a theme that you like and do some due diligence. Now another site that we recommend is called creative market dot com. This creative market dot com. So if you go here and you type in Woo commerce as I've done earlier you will see it says one thousand three hundred design assets. So is actually a little bit more than in vato creative market is fantastic. Not only does what does it have themes it has a lot of other things as well. Now as you scroll down you can see a lot of different themes a lot of pink a lot of purple. I will say creative market is a lot more geared towards women and businesses that cater to women fashion beauty arts and crafts and things like that. Not a it necessarily say that those are geared 100 percent towards women. Those could be men as well but creative market is in my opinion I would rank this number one. I would say in vato number two and then the rest follows because create a market I feel like their designs are really well laid out so. So this is definitely another site that you can look at same methods. Take a look at the theme if you like it. Take a look at the vendor look at the comments. Look at the ratings. Make sure it adds all up before you buy a theme. I can't tell you the countless of times where we spent hundreds and like thousands of dollars on themes only to realize that the theme just didn't work out of the box. So that's why I say it's a matter of looking for a theme and doing your due diligence.

## General Settings Overview

we're going to talk about the general settings of Wu commerce. Now before we talk about that I want to show you the basics of installing and Wu commerce and of course getting your Wu commerce theme. We talked about Wu commerce themes in the previous but I assume that at this point you have it on hand. OK. So first things first you want to log into your WordPress administrator dashboard . So next up we want to go to plug ins ad new click upload plug in and of course you're going to see box . So what you're going to do is down you're going to type in the keyword Woo commerce. Now if you've already downloaded Wu commerce the plug in. You can also choose file install now and go through route . But the simplest route is simply to type in the keyword. Next up click install. Now once that's uploaded all you need to do next is simply click on activate. So we'll wait just a second and once it's activated it is good to go. Now before we can complete it's activated. We need to go through the Wu commerce setup process which basically just entails the basics of your site. So it says the following wizard will help you configure your store that you can get quickly up and running. So you know you fill in your location your country your address your city your state your zip code what currency do you want the payments to be in. What types of products do you plan to sell and more. So next is the payment processors . So basically how are you going to take payments by default . We have a stripe and we have PayPal stripe is free and it's a way that you can take credit card payments. So as you can see accept debit credit cards and so forth. Now stripe I definitely would recommend because if you don't have this you would have to have PayPal and if you have PayPal you automatically assume that people have a PayPal account. Now that is not always the case. That might be the case in tier one countries but beyond that some countries are not allowed to have PayPal. So with that in mind where you want to do next is simply to check box and then type in an email address. So if you haven't had a stripe account created before all you have to do is go ahead and enter email address and the system will actually go and create an account for you via a stripe but of course if you don't necessarily know now you can simply uncheck box. Click on to continue and of course you can go back later down the road click on continue. Next we have shipping. So shipping is mainly required if you have physical products. If you have digital products you can simply skip process. But if you have physical products you're definitely going to need to fill this out. So it says we've created two shipping zones for the United States in the rest of the world. So down here we can set the flat rate if we want to do that and the flat rate for other zones. So you can do that click continue and of course if you're not sure right now you can simply enter zero and do it later down the road and of course next. After that we have the recommended activate and ready OK. So the recommended for all will commerce store simply are different features and options that you can have. They're not necessarily required for you to have. So for example it says store front theme if you want to integrate the initial theme we just call a store front. You can do that if you have a different theme. However you're going to want to uncheck that. Now this is automated taxes. It's got commerce admin so you can manage your stores reports MailChimp. Now you're not going to want to have this if you have your own e-mail auto responder service. So for example if you use active campaign or get response or a waiver you're going to want to uncheck that. And of course it says Facebook enjoy all Facebook products combine into one extension pixel tracking catalogs sync Messenger Chat and all the above. So you can check if you want to. But in my opinion I would simply uncheck most of them and move forward. OK. So we're going to click on continue because I automatically assume that you're going to have a different wordpress theme. So after we click continue the next step is to activate and we're almost done. So it says connect your store to jet pack in my opinion however don't install jet pack because it has a lot of things that you don't necessarily need. So we're going to click skip this step. So it says the next step is to create some products which we'll talk about in just a minute. I'll show you that later and everything is ready so let's go ahead and click on View dashboard and let's just go back to the work press administrator dashboard so to access the Wu commerce plug. Products are located under a different sidebar option called products. They're not located under the Wu commerce section. we're going to talk more about this section right now in terms of installation of the theme. I want to show you that right now before we move forward the wordpress theme is going to be installed under appearance. So if you have to go to an appearance and then themes and then you'll need to find the theme either by adding new click upload a theme choose file find the file click install now and go from there. So that's what you would most likely do if you have a Wu commerce theme that is separate and you've purchased that via maybe theme forest via creative market and more. OK so in this case we've already installed the theme. In fact it's a free theme called Delhi. So what I'm going to do is click activate and here we go. So the theme has been installed and we're good to go now. Different wordpress themes for Wu commerce will be different. So it really depends. So I can't really show you the theme that we're using because it's going to look totally different than ours but the basics are. Once you've installed the Wu commerce theme you can simply go to customize and of course customize the header footer the images and more and a lot of times the WordPress will commerce theme will come with documentation to walk you through step by step as to how you can customize that particular theme. Now that out of the way let's go back to commerce. So if you look at Commerce initially you're going to see the performance reports the charts and more. So we can see the date range. So as you begin to make more sales you'll begin to see more data So that's why it's empty right now because we haven't actually launched an actual shop but this gives us a good idea of what is selling what is not selling and what our customers really want. So that you can focus on that. So if you go under orders we don't see any orders right now but when we receive orders you'll need to just go to do commerce orders and you'll see them all in terms of coupon codes. If you've created a product and you want to create a coupon code then. You can create your first coupon light so you can enter a custom coupon code if you want to or you can simply click on generate coupon code and it'll generate a random coupon code for you. So you could do that or you could type in something like Black Friday maybe 50 saying 50 percent off something like that. So it's really up to you. You can either do customized or you can do random. Now if you scroll down it says General discount type. It's a fixed card discount meaning it's a one time percent discount maybe 50 percent which can vary dependent on how much somebody actually buys and then fixed product discount. So the difference between card discount and product discount is product discount is only focused on a very specific product whereas a fixed card discount is focused on everything that is in the card. Obviously if you choose that then what we need to do is let's say we're going to do a coupon count of 50 dollars and you can either specify that you want the coupon to expire or you can leave it blank if you don't want it to expire so uses restriction basically restricts how many times a coupon can be used. Now because it's a product based coupon code we want to make sure that we select the products. But obviously in this case we don't have any products created. But you're simply going to select the product so once you add the products you'll be able to see the products that are located. You can also exclude products that you don't want to be included within the coupon you can enter maybe a whole category has a coupon code and you exclude categories if you want to so that's basically all that is. they're fairly simple to use and usage limits how many times the coupon can be used can it be useful unlimited times or can it only be used maybe a hundred times until it expires. So that's how to utilize coupons. Next up we have reports. So we're going to go ahead and click on leave. So this is very similar to the orders is going to show the orders the customers and the stock sales by date sales by product sales by category coupons dot by date and customer downloads. So this gives you a better breakdown of what is actually happening within your store. Next up we have settings so within settings this is basically what we dealt with initially. So remember we got General we have shipping we have payments we have accounts we have more. So the main difference is with the wizard and what we see are the products and this is the actual shop page. So it's shop. And then of course we have e mails and what this means are these are e-mails that are sent to the customer such as reset password new account order on hold processing order so you can change these if you want to but you don't have to. But it's nice to have to just start off right off the bat and that's it. Now let's move on to the next page and talk about how to go about creating brand new products or adding products to the system.

## Product Settings Overview

we're going to talk about how to edit the product settings and of course how to create a product. It's super easy All you have to do is go into products which is normally under Woo commerce. So if you created products you'll see of them at the moment. We have no products so that we see create product. So ad new is similar to create a product categories tags and attributes. Now I'll talk about categories and tags and of course product attributes as well. But for now let's just talk about and focus purely on these two right here. So to create a product there are two different ways you can either import them by utilizing this let's say for example that you have 100 different products and creating individual products over and over and over again is just going to take a lot of time. So to do that you can either click Create product or start import . I'm going to go ahead and click Create product but I also opened a different tab with the import products. Now says this tool allows you to import or merge product data to your store via a CSP file or spreadsheet file. All you have to do is populated import it and you're good to go. Now I'm not going to focus a lot on this. This is more advanced what we're gonna do over here and create a new product so this could be let's say book one and then what you want to do is you want to add your description and ideally put them in bullets bulleted points or no bullets whatever. So something like that and of course down you can actually put the price so says product data simple product. So if you're just adding one product it's going to be a simple product. Now you also want to specify is it virtual or is it downloadable. It says virtual products are intangible and are not shipped downloadable products give access to a file upon purchase. So if you're trying to sell let's say for example an e-book or a video it's going to be downloadable. All right. If it's not it will be virtual. So if it's physical of course you want to leave these unchecked. Now if you do downloadable it gives you the option to add a file like in a PDA or a video course or something. But if you want to enter the URL you would need to have some sort of extension that allows you to integrate digital products. But for now to keep it simple you can simply upload the file and of course it says download limits and download expiry. So after that you can go to inventory and has the SDK you if you have something like a physical product you can put in stock status in stock at a stock or on back order sold individually. And of course shipping shipping is only needed if you have a physical product. If you have a digital product is definitely not needed linked products like UPS sells or cross sells meaning things that are related but you can get people to buy more basically. So cross-sell on the other hand would be something that is related. So let's say for example that you are selling something like a water filtration system across all could be something related to that such as maybe the filters or a different type of something that is actually needed. Of course you can scroll down and enter the product description now attributes will focus on that at a later page. But for now that's the basics of adding a product now to the right hand side. You can also add categories product tag which we'll talk about later but you also want to set a product image so whatever enticing image that you have describing that product you'll want to upload it right and of course once you're done you can simply click on publish now. So we'll say regular price is 30 dollars sale price is about 10 dollars and we will simply click Publish and we are good to go.

# Product Organization

we're going to talk about how to organize your products. So as you begin to add more and more products over the course of weeks months or even years things are going to become disorganized is going to be very hard for you to find. And of course your customers to find unless you have a system in place initially. And of course in the long term to make things easier to find . So that's what we're going to talk about in this particular article. And to do that there are several different options that you can take. Now as we mentioned earlier we have categories we have tags in of course we have attributes the attributes are a little bit different. So we're gonna focus mainly on categories and tags. Now you can also access them via the right hand side bar of each and every single one of your products. So on the right hand side you can see product categories and of course you can see product tax. Now it's going to be the same thing except for this location is going to show you all of your categories and of course all of your tax whereas this one over here this allows you to specify how this product is categorized in a category or within the tags. So if we go to product categories you can see a list and of course when you see product tags you're going to see a list. Now it's a good idea to have it written down on paper or have an idea of where things fit and to try to create those product categories ahead of time and then create the product tags ahead of time. So as you begin to add your products you're not thinking of categories when you're adding products but instead you have the categories already created. So let's create an example here let's say for example that we want to create products and focus on products in a specific niche and let's say for example that niche is about water filtration. So if we take a look at different categories we have maybe water filters or we can just say filters. Let's say that the whole site is about water filtration. So we have filters and we just the slug is going to be the user friendly your version. So you can say something like water dash filters and then you'll want to put a description now of course you also want to upload a thumbnail if you can. If you can't no big deal just create a category. So when you're done all you have to do is click on add new category and you're done. Now let's say you've created other categories. To the right we see count the reason why zero is because there's no products that are attached to that product category. Now if we go over and we're going to refresh the page I actually click on update and go from there. And we see filters. And there we go. So if I click on update and I go back to the product categories and I refresh the page from page you'll see that it says filters count 1. So to get a broader view of things you can always go to product categories and see how many products are within white category. The same thing holds true with product tags you can create product tags over or you can simply create them over so let's say for example that we're going to create the product tags over. So this is a water filtration device so we can say something like filters. And you can click enter and then something like water. It's a one year warranty now when you click on update even though we created the product tags on location over they will appear under the tags over. So as you can see it says filters when your warranty water. Count 1 1 and 1 meaning there's one product within this tag. So I wanted to show you that. So that allows you to see that you can create tags and categories via the product section and also within the product tag section and within the product categories section. So that's how easy and simple it is to create an organized system for your products.

# Product Attributes

we're going to talk about product attributes. Now here's what I mean by product attributes to give you the best example. I'm going to go to a site called Alibaba dot com. I did a search for a T-shirt. T-shirts are a great example of this. So you have size and you have color underneath size we have things like small medium large color we have all sorts of different colors. Now what I want you to understand is these are the attributes of size is the attribute color is the attribute. These are what we call values. Now the reason why I'm telling you this is because that is what it's called under which commerce. let's just refresh page you can do it of two of different ways. You can go under attributes and add them there or you can add them on the actual product that you're editing. I like to do it on the product that I'm editing because I can add the values and other attributes you can only add the attributes. So think of attributes kind of like a category of product attributes. So we have color and size since we're dealing with like water filters. We can have size so you pick and choose the attribute you click on add and then you of course you're going to see values. So the values for size would be something like small and then you type that in and then you click add new and then we can type in medium and of course large plug add new into that click OK and that's it. That is how to add a product attribute. Now of course if it were color let's say color you would do the same thing let's say we have Brown you can click on add new look at new green click add new white and we click save attributes. So now we can click update and there we go. So we go under attributes. We can see that we have large medium small under color. We have a variety of different colors and that's it.

# Expansion

we're going to talk about how to expand beyond the core foundation of commerce. So what I mean by that is how do you go from setting up a site let's say for example that you want to sell subscriptions a monthly subscription you want to set up a membership site or you want to integrate with a payment process or beyond just pay Powell or stripe. So to do that in you will need to have an extension. So to do that well you'll need to do is go to woo commerce dot com that's Woo commerce dot com and you'll need to go under the extensions store. Now there are a lot of free extensions but there are a lot that costs money and it's easy to want to pick and choose every single one of them. But the goal is to pick and choose what you need. So under here you can see all new developed by Wu which means it's actually developed by the Wu commerce team because some of these are actually programmed by third party people. We have enhancements such as card check out features merchandising product page features search and navigation and international. We've got marketing email marketing multi-channel marketing promotions reporting and social media marketing. We've got payments in terms of fraud detection in person payments offsite onsite preorders subscriptions and more. So a lot of people tend to run subscriptions. So we have product type shipping store management and subscriptions. So subscriptions has its very own category. But if we click on all you'll be able to see all of the extensions. So says stripe accept all major depth in credit cards. We actually have this. And if you scroll down we can see the most popular are subscriptions bookings and memberships. Now you won't really need bookings unless you have a business model that takes in bookings such as appointments reservations and more. Now if we scroll down we have things like Facebook. We've got Amazon pay as a payment processor. Square pay fast as different payment processors. We've got reporting like Google Analytics. We've got ship station which is a type of software that allows you to ship out physical products and automate that whole process. So if you're dealing with physical products you could do that. We have MailChimp so there are a lot of different extensions that you can buy. But the goal here is not to get lost into them but to figure out what you really need. So if we're trying to set up a subscription and what I would do is up at the top I would type in subscription. Now there is already a category over on subscriptions but I just want to show you as an example if you do a search you'll get an idea of what extensions actually relate to what you want. So you can enter a different keyword that fits you. So we can see subscription downloads newsletter subscription a Weber subscriptions gifting. So for example if you want to set it up so that people can buy like a voucher or a gift subscription and give it to somebody else that's actually a really good idea we've got other payment processors and we got zap and we'll talk more about zap in the next page where we talk about automation. So Zappia is a platform that allows you to automate a lot of Web commerce or WordPress tasks and we'll talk more about other plugins that we have tested that work really well that fit that description so the goal is to figure out what I would do is go through figure out exactly what you need. Write it down and then look at it and ask yourself Do you really need these items. Because it's really easy as I said to get lost in them and try to buy 10 or even 20 different extensions. So start with the basics and then branch off from there. Now if you go under marketing this will actually help you expand your business in terms of marketing like social and it'll help you get more traffic back to your e-commerce site. Now you can also find other ways commerce extensions if you go to Google dot com and search for that. But what I would say is to try to stick with the ones first before you try other extensions and mainly because woo commerce and their team they do a really good job in terms of vetting and trying to figure out what extensions are actually legit and which ones are rated well and have provide really good customer service. Because to get embedded into the directory they're not just going to accept everyone. All right. So that's the point I'm trying to make. And now you know how to expand your business by getting extensions. Let's move on to the next page and talk about well commerce automation.

# WooCommerce Automation

we're going to be talking about how to automate your woo commerce tasks. So there are some tasks that you just need to automate immediately after somebody purchases or perhaps when somebody comes to your site or add something to your shopping cart. So there are two different avenues that you can take. No one is happy ever that Z a p e r dot com Zappia has what we call zaps or automation processes. So if something happens then something else happens. So for example if somebody purchases. Then you can add them to your email list or when they purchase. Not only do you add them to your email list but you also send them an email. You can also do something like if they add something let's say for example to the cart. But they do not purchase but they've signed up. Then you can trigger something to email them. And if they don't respond let's say within 72 hours you could email them 10 percent discount coupon. So there are a variety of things that you can do in terms of Zap. Now I just want to show you as an example if you go to zap year and you log in and you type in Woo commerce. Here are just some of the many different ideas that you can implement. So for example it says save new Web commerce orders to Google Sheets rows add new commerce customers to active campaign as new contacts update contacts inactive campaigns based on new commerce orders.

So if customer a comes and then they get added let's say to active campaign and they purchase product number one now and then it gets updated and lets say a month later they purchase product number two three four. That will basically update the system as well so not only that it's not just all about email marketing you can add them to let's say for example your cookbooks your tax records your accounting bookkeeping you can create cello cards based on the new commerce orders maybe you have a team that needs to take a look at what the orders are. You need to automate the process you need to make it easier for them. So as I scroll down you can see the many different automation processes and tasks that you can implement. So another one you can say add new Woo commerce orders to go to webinar as registrants. So we keep scrolling down. You can see there are hundreds of zaps or automation tasks just for Woo commerce. Now in addition to Zappia Broadcom there is another plug in an actual WordPress plugin. So Zappia is not a plug in it's it's actually a Web site a SaaS platform as you would say. But if you wanted to do more than that there's a nice little plug in called the uncanny auto her WordPress plugin. And this plug in is something that you would install directly into your WordPress platform. So zap you're on the other hand would work outside of your WordPress site. So for example the uncanny automate . The reason why it's really unique is because it integrates with a lot of different WordPress plugins that are not inside of Zappa air sizing and see you can automate all of these between each other. So for example Woo commerce. You can have something that says if somebody purchases an online course through commerce then they get added to let's say for example learn dash which is a platform or WordPress plugin that allows you to sell online courses now to just give you some ideas. If we go to all triggers and actions if we scroll down you can see that there are a variety of different triggers. So a trigger means something that happens beforehand before something else can happen. So if this happens then do this. So that's what a trigger is. And then the action is what happens after the trigger initiates so have gamma press. We have gravity forms and more. So for example you could say OK if somebody fills out a form Gravity Forms and you have that WordPress plug in you could say if somebody's a user submits a form or a user submits a form that contains a very specific value. Then do this or do that maybe add them to an online course or maybe add them to your membership site or maybe create a pop up or add them to your events calendar. There are so many different triggers and actions that you can create with the uncanny automaker. This is a WordPress plugin that we've tested and we've really liked and it's definitely worth it. Now in terms of cost if you go to the main site you click on buy automaker. You can see that there are a variety of recipes that you can create. Now the main difference between a Zappia dot com and this plug in is that with this plug in you can create unlimited actions and unlimited recipes was happy air on the other hand you do have a limited amount of what we call zaps or trigger and actions. So with this one you can create a limited whereas with the Zap here you have a limit of that. But on the other hand zap the air also provides access to over 15 hundred apps whereas the uncanny auto maker really focuses in hones in on WordPress plugins. So these two systems we highly recommend we use we've tested and we've really enjoyed using them. There are many other sites out there that do this kinds of things but we've really narrowed it down to these two sites and you can access the uncanny automated by going to automate our plug in dot com that's automated plug in dot.com or he can simply go to Google dot com and do a search for the uncanny automated.

www.ingramcontent.com/pod-product-compliance
Lightning Source LLC
Chambersburg PA
CBHW050322220526
45465CB00005B/2087